Embers & Whispers

Clementine Jasmine-Rae

BookLeaf
Publishing

Presentation by *BookLeaf Publishing*

Web: www.bookleafpub.com

E-mail: info@bookleafpub.com

ISBN:

First edition 2023

To my beautiful children, my Queen & my grandchild

ACKNOWLEDGEMENT

To my beloved friends, my Queen and, at times reluctantly, life - which has given me the opportunity to write from those experiences and provide joy and peace to others

She is

She's not just my girl
Shes my home
My rest
My heart
and my safe space

I see you

I see your flaws
and I love them,
I see your strengths
and I love them,
I see your looks
and I love them,
I see your demons,
and I love them,
I see your thoughts
and I love them

I see you
and
I love you

Requirements

I'm at a point in my life
where I no longer have expectations
I have requirements.

Respect my time
Match my effort
Keep your word
Always be honest
Stay consistent

Those are my requirements
Not my expectations

Cold damp sheets

Rambling inconsistent thoughts
Cold damp sheets
Facing deep demons
Whilst you sleep

A punchered heart
A tired, weary soul
Rambling inconsistent thoughts
As I slowly weep

Shattered ideas of love
Drawing my last breath
Slipping deeper and deeper
As my eyes slide shut

Kindness

Without kindness, we would be monochrome
Muted
Mere imitations of ourselves
Missing that which makes us .... us
Devoid of our vibrancy
Of our uniqueness
Through which our soul soars.

Without kindness, we would be
Dulled
Shrivelled back
A shell
Empty at the very core

Your name

Oh your name

Its the strongest negative and
positive connotation in all language

It either lights me up
or leaves me aching all over for days

Gaslighting

He spins words and gravity
and turns her actions
until he world is tipping
plunging over its own axis.

In his narrative
Light is dark
and peace is chaos

He creates a dark room
for her
That she now calls shelter
decievingly comforted by her worse enemy-
invisible to her.

Internal Pain

Underneath her smile
There is a brave strength
Understand her blue eyes
There is a ocean built from a million tears shed
Underneath her soft skin
There are so many scars and bruises

You can not see the pain
Not from the outside
Only traces of scars
Performed by her own hand

She can't and won't trust you anymore
Because of what you have made her feel
She can not love you anymore
Because to feel what she feels
Will only weaken her strength
and open wounds...

...which will never heal

Beauty

There is nothing more amazing and beautiful
than a person
Who is doing the hard work
Healing open wounds
Trying to stem the pain.

And figuring out who they really are

Little Girl

It was time to feel it all
Knowing the journey had been ignored
For far too long
The pit of her stomach
Wretched in angst and fear.

Shallow breaths increasing
Heart racing
Hands shaking
Her body remembering

In a effort to soothe the angst
She focused on the in and out of her breath
The pace
The depth
The rise of her chest
Inhaling deeply
Slow release
The mantra melody begins...

"You are alright right now"
"You are safe right now"
"You are alright right now"
"You are safe right now"

Repeatative in words and rhythm

14/09/23

She's sat there torn between
Running and staying
The duvet begs her to lie back down
and be enveloped in sleep
The head
The head so tired
Begs her to run and end it all.

Emotions replaced with a tidle wave
Of numbness
She dressed on autopilot
She writes letters of love and pain
and she slowly walks out into the darkness.

An accomplice

The cable
Such a innocent object in life,
Becomes her escape.
The tree,
So beautiful in nature,
Becomes her accomplic.

The cable tightens and all she feels is relief,
The pain in her heart,
Replaced with physical pain.

The end is near.
The pain will end.

Why are you upset?

Are you upset with the hand
that did not take yours when you reached out?

Or, are you upset with yourself,
For reaching out to someone who had no
intention of staying ?

Rainbows

That girls rainbow after her storm
Is what makes you keep chasing
her in the rain

True Colours

Is not their true colours
that you suddenly see
Their true colours
we're always there.
It is your eyes that coloured them in kindness.

Healing

Healing comes
When they come looking
for the old you...

Pushing buttons
Pulling triggers
But, they can't you.

Dont question

Just sit
Don't ask
Don't question
Let me sit enveloped
In your safe silence.

Just sit
Dont ask

Just once more

The initial hit
Forever chasing
Veins flowing
Eyes dilating

Company is suddenly enticing
Fuel is denied,
Suddenly unnecessary

Just one more line
One more tab
One more needle

I promise
It will be the last.

Baby girl ...please listen

Baby girl
The silence is in his reply
Listen closely
He says everything
When he says nothing.

Sacred space

I think more clearly
Amongst the tired and broken gravestones
When the day is done
and the world feels heavy
I seek you out
I quietly ask permission to share your sacred
space.

It fills me with such calm
Confirms that everything is going to be okay
and I am where I need to be.

As I turn to leave
I give silent but meaningful thanks
For the role you played
Albeit unknowingly

Printed in Great Britain
by Amazon

36563237R00020